BAD ENGINE

ALSO BY MICHAEL DENNIS

quarter on it's edge (Fast Eddie Press, 1979)

sometimes passion, sometimes pain (Ordinary Press, 1982)

no saviour and no special grace (South Western Ontario Poetry, 1983)

how to keep a poet out of jail – or ship of fools, car of idiots (privately published, 1985)

poems for jessica-flynn (Not One Cent of Subsidy Press, 1986)

so you think you might be judas (privately published, 1987)

wayne gretzky in the house of the sleeping beauties (Lowlife Publishing, 1988)

Fade to Blue (Pulp Press, 1988)

Portrait (Dollarpoems/Brandon University, 1988)

what we remember and what we forget (Bobo Press, 1993)

missing the kisses of eloquence (General Store, 1994)

the on-going dilemma of small change (above/ground, 1995)

what we pass over in silence (above/ground, 1996)

no gravy, no garlands, no bright lights (privately published, 1999)

This Day Full of Promise (Broken Jaw Press, 2002)

All Those Miles Yet to Go (LyricalMyrical Press, 2005)

Poems for Another Poetry Reading (LyricalMyrical, 2006)

Arrows of Desire (General Store, 2006)

Coming Ashore on Fire (Burnt Wine Press, 2009)

Watching the Late Night Russian News in the Nude (Burnt Wine Press, 2009)

on being a dodo (Burnt Wine Press, 2009)

forgiveness, my new sideline (Proper Tales Press, 2009)

Smile (Burnt Wine Press, 2009)

how are you she innocently asked (Apt. 9 Press, 2010)

The Uncertainty of Everything (Burnt Wine Press, 2011)

A Tiresome Litany of Indignities (Proper Tales Press, 2014)

Talking Giraffes (Phafours, 2015)

BAD ENGINE
New & Selected Poems

MICHAEL DENNIS

anvil
PRESS

Anvil Press Publishers Inc.
P.O. Box 3008, Main Post Office
Vancouver, B.C. V6B 3X5 Canada
www.anvilpress.com

Library and Archives Canada Cataloguing in Publication

Dennis, Michael, 1956-
[Poems. Selections]
      Bad engine : new & selected poems / Michael Dennis.

ISBN 978-1-77214-077-4 (softcover)

      I. Title. II. Title: Poems. Selections.

PS8557.E563B33 2017   C811'.54   C2017-901250-9

Printed and bound in Canada

Editor for the press: Stuart Ross
Cover design by Rayola.com
Cover art: "Packed Pictures" by Kaye Wong
Typesetting: Stuart Ross
Author photo: Kirsty Jackson

Represented in Canada by Publishers Group Canada
Distributed by Raincoast Books

The publisher gratefully acknowledges the financial assistance of the Canada Council for the Arts, the Canada Book Fund, and the Province of British Columbia through the B.C. Arts Council and the Book Publishing Tax Credit.

For K.

CONTENTS

INTRODUCTION

Michael Dennis lives, breathes and perhaps smokes poetry. In a sense, he is the ultimate occasional poet. Well, he writes constantly, so I don't mean occasional in that way. Michael is a poet who writes to mark events: from the most minor to the most catastrophic. We are humans responding humanly whether we are facing either of those experiences, and I sense that Michael feels a moral — or maybe artistic — responsibility to lay his cards on the table, whatever he's facing.

Michael is also a people's poet, a populist poet: you don't need a graduate degree to read his work, and you're not going to miss anything. You don't read a Michael Dennis poem and say, "Well, that went right the hell over my head." Though sometimes his poems may *hit* you in the head.

What is the greatest appeal in Michael's work? I'd say it is his conviction, his directness. And as brave and no-bullshit as he usually is, he's the first to admit to his own fuck-ups. Here is one of us: a human, but telling it like it is — like it is for him.

Michael belongs to a tradition of poets who do exactly these things, in their different ways: Charles Bukowski, of course, and Lyn Lifshin; Milton Acorn, Tom Wayman and Al Purdy; Eileen Myles and Sharon Olds. To me, a surrealist/absurdist, it's a precarious path to walk, because, well, it's so *raw*. But that also means that to successfully pull off such a poem is a pretty mean feat.

When we embarked on this volume of selected and new poems, at various times I nudged Michael to take a dip into surrealism, or experimentalism; I gave him assignments to get him to produce cut-ups. I could tell his heart wasn't in it, though, and why would it be? For him, perhaps there is enough surrealism, absurdism, and disjunctiveness in real life. Besides, Michael *has* experimented: there are some visual poems in his early books, but it clearly wasn't a route he was interested in following.

It's worth noting, though, that when Michael and I have collaborated — and we've written well over a hundred poems together — he doesn't hesitate to go totally weird on me, just as I'm trying to get more normal to accommodate him. Perhaps it's that dynamic of collaboration — because you don't take full responsibility for the poem, you are willing to go wild...or go realist. Have a look at our half-dozen or so poems in my collection of collaborations with 29 Canadian poets, *Our Days in Vaudeville* (Mansfield Press, 2015), and in our forthcoming *Dagmar One One One*, when we find a publisher for it.

In collaborative work, Michael seems to leave behind intention — intention, that is, to do anything but write a collaborative poem. In his solo work, meanwhile, Michael seems intent on telling a particular story, making a point, expressing a lament, or simply saying, "I mean, isn't this fucked?" That's whether he's talking about some dumb racist he met on a houseboating trip, an inane job on the assembly line he's found himself stuck in, a ridiculously complex relationship with a lover, or abuse at the hands of an uncle.

Michael and I have been friends since the early 1980s, when he found me on the street in downtown Toronto selling my self-published poetry and fiction chapbooks. We've been close friends ever since, as he's moved — with a few detours along the way — from Toronto to Peterborough to Ottawa, the city he's made his home now for over thirty years. He's the author of a dozen books, from a variety of publishers, and countless chapbooks and broadsides.

He once published a book to raise enough money to spring himself from jail. He has traded readings for meals and for art. His love of contemporary visual art — and the astonishing breadth of that love's range — fills the house he shares with his wife, Kirsty.

Michael also has one of the best private poetry collections I've ever seen, and I get the feeling he's read most of the books in the tiny study where he ingeniously keeps finding new space to add book-shelves (an imperative since he began his practice of writing about a book of poems he likes every two days on his *Today's book of poetry* blog). Only sporadically employed these past few years, Michael was looking for a way to feed his poetry addiction, and once he got that blog going, the books starting pouring in. Over the phone, he sometimes sounds pretty pissed off if only a book or two arrive in a given week. Now, with that blog, he's working practically full-time in the service of poetry.

As to the editing of these pieces, well: I remember when Michael was going to read his legendary "hockey night in canada" poem at the opening night of the Ottawa International Writers' Festival nearly twenty years ago. He was on the bill with Pierre Berton and Pierre Berton's bow tie and a couple of other big-time writers. Michael showed me the epic poem in manuscript form, and I said, "Over here, where you mention this guy holding a drink, why don't you specify it's a beer?" He glared at me and ignored me. How dare I meddle with his first thought/best thought? Meanwhile, that night at the packed National Arts Centre auditorium, the crowd rose to its feet for Michael's mile-a-minute poem. In auditoriums, cafés, living rooms, bars, galleries, and even sex shops, Michael's plain-spoken approach to the human condition connects with audiences.

It was many years later that Michael sent me a little batch of new poems. I couldn't help myself. I dug in and condensed, and chopped out the philoso-phizing. The stories were so good, the POV, the gut jab: he didn't need to *explain*. I asked him, a little uncertainly, if he wanted to see my suggested edits. To my surprise, first, he said sure, and second, he said they were pretty good.

And so *Bad Engine* offers up revised versions of just about all the selected poems, as well as a big com-plement of recent works. The couple thousand poems I read to concoct this mixture drove home to me that Michael Dennis is the real thing when it comes to poetry without artifice: poetry delivered directly from the various organs of the gut.

As for that drink in "hockey night in canada" — it's still a drink, not a beer. Michael was absolutely right on that count.

Stuart Ross
Highway 7 to Ottawa
October 2016

NEW POEMS

my mother and I sat waiting for death

my mother and I sat waiting for death
we both assumed
he'd be coming for my mother
and we were right

we sat on the kitchen chairs
my father had upholstered
when my baby sister Judy was born
we sat there and watched the arms of the clock
chase each other
as the sun went round the earth
and the cat outside
circled the house
secure in the not knowing
that death was waiting

most of my mother was tired
and ready
she understood
there was no turning back

she wasn't eager to meet death
but in the end, he couldn't come fast enough
as the sun set and then rose
just like every other day
somewhere a cloud, some rain
another place flowers

the limitless sky

we had rented a houseboat in the Kawarthas
docked at Lovesick Lake
where others had tied their boats for the night

we had just finished our dinner when
neighbours invited us to their fire
six of us, all adults
drinking beer and wine
as the darkness came across the water
and snuffed out the light

the conversation started as most do with strangers
but we were all from the same
small part of the world
from the colour of our skin
we might all have been cousins
and then

Bob from Ajax began talking "sand jockeys," "Pakis"
we were on a spit of land between two lakes
and several hours of darkness away from escape

my wife knew me and hoped I'd choose silence
but as the beer dwindled, Bob's bravado blossomed
I could not help myself

my wife's eyes tensed in the glow of the fire
I waited for Bob to pause
and then said
             Bob
I couldn't possibly disagree with you more
there are several things wrong with your argument
and if you'll give me a minute
I'll explain them to you

the owls in the trees hooted silent, the mice quit stirring
I had Bob's full attention

you know what I said
I said it as politely as I could
then we picked up our chairs
thanked everyone for their hospitality
and walked back to our dark boat
I could still hear the crackle of their fire in the distance

in the true dark of a northern Ontario night
I looked up into the sky and saw the history of time
in the millions of visible stars
dawn was breaking in another part of the world
where other unreasonable people
do unreasonable things
while most get out of bed
hope the best for themselves
and everyone else
under the limitless sky

in the backyard

a lie is a lie
is sitting on your couch
eating out of the cat's dish
hiding in the backyard
between
garbage cans

how to raise a bitter child

it helps
if you start early
with disappointments

be stingy with love
and with food

go hard on anger
teach the hard lesson often

enforce it with
the iron hand of the vengeful

be so caught up in the horrors
and lost in the demons
of your own childhood
that you are incapacitated

always best
to take away hope
at an early age

never give the child
something to look forward to:
forward
is the wrong
direction

last words before I put a bullet in my brain

I'm so fucking tired
of waking up in pain every day
I absolve myself of everything
it's too late to be sorry now
and in ten minutes
I am never going to be sorry again

to those I have caused grief
I wish I had been better
to those who hurt me
I hope you didn't mean it

I am far too young to be this tired
I am guilty of everything you say
from this moment on

it's so hard to know what is true

dogs bark their barky bark
and cats meow and growl
I've even seen
a cat who could bark like a dog
when the occasion called for it
although she felt guilty about it
when discovered

it was the first time I saw
that animals are liars too

Meeting the Duke

I just got a dragonfly stoned
not the behaviour one expects
from a man nearing sixty, but fuck it

all four wings of the transparent giant fluttered
when the first waft of blue smoke
rolled over his compound eyes
he didn't seem to mind
so I shared the rest of my joint
with my new-found helicopterfriend

we were both on the deck of a cottage
on a quiet lake on a quiet day
we both watched the water below us
flat as liquid gets, the wind dead

I doubt we were looking
for the same things
but you never know

eventually he turned toward me
or at least toward the smoke
Duke was what I named him
as he flew away sideways

flowers never die

"Flowers never die. Heaven is whole.
But ahead of us we've only somebody's word."
– Osip Mandelstam

when we were in New Orleans
the old woman at the corner store
told us
"bullets don't know your name,
don't care who you are"

the night before
bullets had flown like heavy rain
around the abandoned house next door

the police arrived like bright neon flies
as we skittered under the furniture

the next morning
we headed for Baton Rouge
to hear Cajun music
we dined bayou
as the band danced the audience
into the floor

one night it's the desperate bullets
of the dispossessed
victims of systemic poverty
indifference, racism, acrimony

the next night
steak and shrimp
every salad you can name

the wrestler

the bees consort
on the purple Russian sage
in our garden
this is what passes for action in my life
several trees away, a cardinal's barking
he's swearing at a crow

the hum of the city is underneath everything
a siren will wail somewhere nearby
then fade into someone else's worst day
while I fold laundry

a woman on our street
has three dogs
but walks them
one at a time

she used to be a wrestler
Mexican-style, with the mask and everything
but won't tell me her story
which is too bad
truth usually kicks the crap out of fiction

coyotes

when he first heard
his uncle
had raped his mother
he almost lost his mind

he wanted them both
back from the grave

missing his mother
was what he was best at

and killing the newly animated carcass
of his lousy uncle
became his new obsession

but the number of angels
that fit on the head of a pin
never changes

all the dancing elephants
in the universe
will tell you so

the trees blowing fall leaves
on your lawn tell you so
the snow falling
as snow is meant to fall
tells you

we can change little
including ourselves
coyotes dwell in the darkness
of every city in the land

The Starlet

I am back in the Windsor
of my motor-line days
and in my old neighbourhood

I am behind the wheel
of one of my stepfather's old Buicks
a light-toned monkey-shit-brown wreck

I am minding my own business
when a famous young tv starlet
walks by my panorama

she says hello like we know each other
and in dream context we do

she gets into my car
closes the back door
as simultaneously
a strange man
taps on my window
asks for me by name
and then without another word
shoots me in the head

I hear the bang
see brain and blood
on the steering wheel
say "that hurt"
and plaintively ask the starlet
"am I dead?"
she replies in her best
sad, famous actress voice
"yes, Michael, you're dead"

she pauses for a second
then tells me, quietly,
that she'll tell my father
the one who owns
the monkey-shit-brown Buick
with my brains on the dashboard

then I woke up
the sheets sweaty
like nightmare sheets are
the morning hours distant
and all those sleepless hours
to get there

the forest

went for a walk on a wooded island
where no one lives
heard a wild turkey in the bush
saw a rainbow
of coloured mushrooms
the sun shone hard
for an early-September mid-morning
and I could hear
a cornucopia of mosquitoes, flies, gnats

nothing has changed for me
I see the beauty
as nature rarely lets anyone down
but it doesn't matter
what I hear on my soundtrack
is my uncle's laughing taunts
the sounds of my childhood
around my ankles in a weep

Delmore Schwartz said

my dead mother appeared in my dreams last night
and I was so happy to see her
she's been dead and dust these twenty-three years
so you can imagine my surprise

whatever joy was quickly abated
by the guy playing me in my dreams
he started yelling at my dead mother
that I'd wasted the opportunity
mortified that I just didn't hug her
and hang on

Delmore Schwartz said
that responsibility begins in dreams
and Delmore
was one clever guy
but the asshole
who played me in my dream last night
won't be invited back
my mother didn't seem
to like him at all

another Christmas carol

the weekend before Christmas
I returned to the town I grew up in
and went to the local hospital
to visit the man who raised me
I'd seen him several weeks ago
and he'd been okay
but since then
he had tumbled headfirst
into his own death wish
he'd quit talking
taken out his teeth
and given up

this man and I
don't share a name
or blood
but I've called him Dad
for fifty years
and when I arrived
and asked if he wanted a visit
he said "no"

knowing it might be our last
I said those things
I wanted him to know
my voice echoed around his room
and I sat there listening to it
until it was time to leave
I kissed his balding head
and watched his eyes
not watching me
and then
walked quiet down the hall

Rock Haven Motor Hotel

she got into my cab at the train station
knew where she wanted to go
a motel just west of the city
I was much younger then
and she seemed lonely

we talked the few miles
talked through red lights and green
and when we arrived at
the Rock Haven Motor Hotel
we were on a first-name basis
and for a tip
she asked me into her room
it was clear what she wanted
and I was willing
but by the time
we were through
it was clear
I didn't have what she needed

she cried while I got dressed
cried some more
when I kissed her goodbye
I closed the door softly
got back in my taxi
turned on the light
let the dispatcher know
I was back in business
rolled the big car softly
over the noisy gravel
and back
out onto the street

Joining the Foreign Legion

suppose you wanted to join
the French Foreign Legion
just like in the movies
all your life
you've desired to be
a man without a past
looked forward
to being without a future

so you sign up
only to find yourself
in a Brechtian world
scripted by the ghost of Genet
and inhabited by the penis-towers
of Rainer Werner Fassbinder's imagination

you are shocked:
in the film you inhabit
the patriarchal representations
of your safe world
have evaporated

in their place, a new horizon
and in this erotic spectacle of masculinity
male bodies become, like Foucault said,
"polymorphous palaces of pleasure"

you have always depended
on the straight world
for representations of masculinity
tried to justify yourself
by reenacting them
never realizing
that masculinity is learned behaviour

you remember the heroic stoicism
of the Legionnaires from *Beau Geste* (1966)
and could never imagine Doug McClure
kissing a man for any reason

but the creatures in
this brave new world
are outside the binary
that once balanced your brain

in this cinema
every conversation questions gender
until biology is just a class
you took back in high school

at the end of Claire Denis's *Beau Travail* (1999)
when Denis Lavant
says his sad goodbye with a bullet
you can hear Fass-
binder cry
on some distant quiet dune
Brad Davis too

all those men marching
that silent army
unseen
by the gaze of all
but a few

When Sally Came for Harry

in the world of passive versus active
Meg Ryan pretending to achieve orgasm
over a deli sandwich
is telling Harry
in no uncertain terms
that the phallus is phony

much to Billy Crystal's wonderment
Sally has taken
all of the power
into her lily-white hands
and without touching herself
dismantles the social construction
of dominance

she fakes
the satisfaction
she'd present a male lover
to keep alive
the illusion of his own prowess

if she — and apparently she does —
controls her own sexuality, her own orgasm
her own joy and satisfaction
she has no real need for cock
except to assuage the need
of the man attached to it

Meg Ryan moaning over coleslaw
in a New York deli
cuts through every illusion
in Billy Crystal's head

Pat Garrett and Lola and Bilidikid

what no one ever seems to talk about
when the Peckinpah gore settles
is that *Pat Garrett and Billy the Kid*
is a good old-fashioned love story

Sheriff Garrett loves Billy so much
he has to kill him to prove it

and sweet Billy
barefoot and tender
loves Garrett
right back
enough to let him
end his days
with the full stop
of a bullet

as Mayakovsky
might have said

*

and in cowboy Berlin
neither Lola nor Bilidikid
can perform themselves
beyond the reality
of the gender
they exhibit

they are as doomed
as gunslingers
who cannot adapt
the old world
spun to the edges

weighed down
by a gender politic
they cannot outdraw

but in the fading sunset
hope emerges

a man can have emotion
and masculinity
Lola's optimistic and resourceful friend
intones "I am a
woman with balls"
and the taxi driver smiles
in bemused flirtation

★

elsewhere
Billy Wilder turns over
in his grave, giggles
remembers Jack Lemmon
on the water
with Joe E. Brown
then turns over again
into the eternally peaceful slumber
we wish upon all our heroes

vanishing point

we were on a country road
and made a wrong turn
it was my fault, I was drunk
and my sober wife was driving
I'd told her to take the turn

the mistake was quickly obvious
the narrow road turned into a dark tunnel
complete overgrowth atop
and the gravel gave way to a dirt path
there was no place to turn around
and as the lane narrowed
I went back in time
to another dark woods
and I panicked

my always sane wife stayed sane
while I had derailed
she did get the car turned

and later that night
as I wrestled against my inky past
my sane wife woke me to stop my screaming
as that dark lane
imposed its vanishing point
on my horizon

snakes with shoes

the grey sky doesn't matter
the snow on the ground doesn't matter
wind coming around the corner doesn't matter
the last red cardinal shivering on that branch doesn't matter
or the broken red wagon with only three wheels

poetry certainly doesn't matter
nor the eulogies for old hockey players
dead at centre ice

you need James Caan as Santino
for any real justice
beating his wife-beating
brother-in-law to a pulp

I know them
and you know them too
the men who hit the women
in their lives

snakes with shoes
they look just like you and me

oblivious or obtuse
they pull their shoes on same as us
one foot at a time

then they walk in winter air
beneath the grey sky
the bitter wind whipping around the corner
as they adjust their scarves
walk by the stranded wagon
walk by the shivering bird

the world weeps for fallen heroes
soldiers, senators, centre-ice men
while the rich eat the dreams of the poor
power fills its own vacuum

but the thing is this:
worms are going to poke out of the earth
and in a house on your block
a man you know
will punch his wife
in the mouth, hard

you'll never hear a word of it

the snore

my wife of twenty years
is snoring beside me
you don't fall in love
because of snoring
or any of the other
innocuous sounds
life brings into marriage
I like to think her snoring
comes from
a deep reservoir of calm
the love sighs of the secure

we are at a lake, it is summer
my wife in repose in a black bathing suit
whispering sibilant greetings
from that place we go to slumber
a code deciphered over two decades
of sharing a pillow

SELECTED POEMS

curved light

for bonnie sheckter

i saw a candle
do cartwheels

pulling horses
through the night

funeral for a fly

with a book of richard brautigan's poetry
i killed an unsuspecting fly
(to be buried later in the envelope
of a letter from my lover's mother)

i had no idea
that poems so short
could carry such weight

sparrow, again

not sure if you'll remember
but about two years ago
i wrote about the bird
at the top of the cement street light
except the street light was in windsor
but today while walking down the street
there was the same bird
i'm dead serious
it was the same bird
i'm sure it's not the same street light
but damn it
it was the same bird

so what i'm thinking is that the bird heard i had moved
and followed

you see today she looked right at me
from the top of the pole
and said something

my bird dictionary is at home

april 29 1979

1

went to see him like i had to
i mean a surprise and everything
and he asked me to write in his book
so i did
but i couldn't write i love you

2

joe was asleep
and they fired the housekeeper
and the old clock
trash of '56
was on the tv

3

and marg's sulking
because michael won't make love
with his guitar
and the lights out
and we made her get cokes at *the exorcist*
while linda blair turned her head around

4

he followed us
pulled us over
checked my licence
asked if we were drinking
then set us free

5

it felt better driving away
than it did driving to

6

except when we went to my father's

tournesol

for carol and ernst

i asked her to come outside
so we could make love
beneath the sun
she turned out the lights
and did impressions of sunflowers

i share an apartment with two artists

so i headed for the bathroom
it had been a long night
of too many beers
the morning sun was screaming in the window
michael, it's time to go
i raced down the hall
to find the window covered with a black sheet
the bathtub full of chemicals
and a developer tray sitting on the toilet
i was desperate
and the sink was handy

i was also in need of a bath
so i emptied the tub
washed down the sulphur smell
and turned on the hot water that would save me

as usual i sank to my chin
got the paper wet while i read the news
amid the steam of the tub
and the odour of the chemicals

when i dried myself off
my skin was its usual post-bath lobster red
i sprinkled myself with baby powder
and got dressed to face the day

as i walked down the stairs and toward the street
i could feel the pictures beginning to develop
on my chest and thighs

why i don't like fellini

imagine a twenty-year-old woman
she is lying on her stomach on the beach
getting a tan
perhaps her back is getting a little too much sun
there are pink lines
where the straps to her top usually cross
the sand is warm and feels good
she is daydreaming:
her arms are around a young man
and they are kissing

she feels a sting on her left cheek
just below her eye
reflex brings her hand to her face
she removes a small black-and-red spider
then shudders and quickly leaves the beach
feeling at her cheek with a testing hand

later that night her cheek is red and swollen
she promises herself
she will see the doctor in the morning
but when she wakes it is gone
there is no pain and no swelling
by afternoon she is in the bar with friends
and has forgotten the entire thing

two months later
while dressing in front of the mirror
she notices a small swelling under her left eye
by midday it is a noticeable lump
and by the following morning
it is a fairly large growth
she touches it constantly
and although there is no pain
her fingers return to it again and again

while she is touching it
it explodes like a boil
instead of spewing forth the expected pus and blood
dozens of small black spiders fly out of her face
as she screams
the spiders continue to empty themselves
from her cheek

several months later
the young woman is still in the hospital
she cannot look in the mirror
cannot bring herself to touch her own flesh
she becomes hysterical at the sight of spiders

in the glass

he goes looking for sympathy
she tells him
to look in the dictionary
between shit and syphilis
he sees her looking out the doorway
where they used to kiss goodnight
he imagines it again in his mind
his sex becomes hard
his face crimson
he tries to say hello
casually
instead he stares
and she laughs

he rips up her letters
spills ink over her phone number
throws her dictionary in the garbage
in the bathroom
his reflection frightens him

breakfast in bed

i am somewhere between
sleep and conversation
my face buried
in pillows
i am lying face down
spread-eagled on the mattress
the sun on my back
it must be a beautiful day

i feel you sit down on the bed
and hear you talking to me
you are peeling an orange
i feel it in my nose
it is the freshest thing i know

it is strong
it wakes me up
it is pure
like the sun
i am awake
i turn over
see you looking at me
say good morning
kiss your knee
ask for a small piece of orange

no saviour and no special grace

what does it matter
i am sitting in my apartment
and looking out the window
at the people going by
it is summer and it is hot
the afternoon means nothing
the people on the street are dying
i am looking down and dying too
the mercury topped a hundred yesterday
and will do it again today
the rent is due
so is my bill at morries
the greasy spoon across the street
they know me there
i have a cheeseburger8
a can or two of coke
say "hey, marg, put it on the bill"
if i have a reading and make a few bucks
i go in and cash my cheque
marg gives me the difference
we get along fine

i see people walking into morries
and coming out the same
hot and confused
i can see in the window
an electric fan rotates slowly
beside the bran muffins and butter tarts
it doesn't make any difference
just moves the hot air around the room
as cars drift by the window
they are doing nothing
just driving around the few blocks downtown
a clever plot by the mayor and his bandits

they've cut off the welfare
and are giving away gas to those with cars
to make it look like the city isn't dying

the only store doing any business
is the sally ann
it used to be only the broke
with holes in their shoes
wandered in the door
but not anymore
there is no pride left
there is nothing
if i had an egg
i could cook it on the danger high voltage sidewalk
and if i had some bacon
i wouldn't be sitting in the window
i'd be over at the king's
listening to the music
and watching one of the ladies
dancing and giving it away
she'd be wrapped in red
she'd be taking it off
but it doesn't matter because i hear them knocking
and they are coming for me
it doesn't even matter who they are
i've got the furniture piled against the door

if they want me
they can come in the windows
or through the roof
and until they do there is the street
with the cars drifting past
they come from somewhere
and go somewhere else

i watch the people go by
sometimes they'll be pretty women or a handsome man
doesn't matter
they are all doomed
they just have further to fall
when the boom comes down
the old women
with plastic bags full of their histories
they will survive if only from habit
but what of the beauty shop queens
who spend tuesdays at the club
when the club closes the doors
and they have nothing left
but to walk by my window
what will they do
they will scream in the streets
and pull their hair
their men will be weak things
crying and pulling at their teeth
there will be no saviour
and no special grace
the end will come
as quickly and surely
as the noon explosion
of the engine of a '63 pontiac
pushed to the limit just once too often
and i'll watch it
the engine blowing on the street below
marg will serve coffee to the bystanders
there will be blood and gasoline on the blacktop
the heat melting them to one
it will be a sign and
the stores will close their doors

where the water tastes like wine

"I'm going where the water tastes like wine
we can jump in the water, stay drunk all the time…"
– Canned Heat

i am looking out the window
it is a car window
the car is moving
the world is speeding by
and i am unsure about dreaming
i am in a dream
going to the water
i hear voices mumble
and turn to concerned faces
knocking to get in
my eyes betray me
everything is unclear and moving
the sky is blue and blurred
i see clouds like pandora's boxes
littering the sky with the problems of man
the voices are calling
i feel a hand on my shoulder
it is a dream
i am looking at myself in the distance
see a hand on my shoulder
and hear the voices knocking
the wine is tasting sweeter
the water coming closer
i see darkness
its crisp edge
winnowing

dinner

halfway through dinner that first night
a guard came over to my table
and asked if it was my first time
and of course I answered yes

he said he thought so and smiled
told me I would get the hang of it
and just to watch
what the others were doing
and I did

where they put their empty trays
and where they put their dishes
trying so hard to fit in
that my being out of place
was the only thing in the room
that was clear to me

the first night

the cell I am sharing
with two other men
is about the same size
as the bathroom
in the house I rent
I am sleeping on the top bunk
the old man has the single
and there is a young man beneath me
both are snoring loudly
and one of them, I am unsure which
has a distinct problem with his feet
they stink

the lights went out
at eleven o'clock
this is my first night in jail
I am on my back
and looking at the ceiling
it is three feet away
it doesn't look any different
from any other ceiling
no different from the ceilings
I have seen
while lying beneath the woman I love
the bed is not uncomfortable
but sleep will not come
I listen to the chorus of snoring
and hear someone in a distant cell singing

this is not the movies
and the singing is not beautiful
I close my eyes and wait
for the sun to come up through the window

Nancy's perfect little gun

what you see when you look in the white house window
is Nancy in jackboots and black leather
she has spurs and a whip and a perfect little smile
Ronnie has on a collar and it is tied to the bed
there is the soft electric hum of a video camera
and an occasional ecstatic whimper from the president
you can barely maintain your grip
but the show is more than worth it
so you hang there by your fingertips
as Nancy delicately lays the whip to his back
not whipping him but teasing
his old bones wither and shake till he chortles
"crack that whip, damn you, crack that whip, you bitch"
she continues to tease him without words
the leather laced across his back like lace
there are red welts from earlier lessons
and then when he suspects it least
she snaps that sucker so hard it breaks the skin
and his scream of agony meaning pleasure
rocks the white house windows
you are still hanging by your fingers
but cannot stifle a laugh
she hears you and the laughter stops
she quicksteps over to the bed
reaches under her pillow
and with her perfect little gun
takes perfect little aim
and blows you
and this story away

fishbowl

the sky is getting dark
people heading home from work
I am sitting in the bookstore window
watching them
it is my job

I watch people
and when I think
they aren't watching me
I write everything down

I like it sitting here
I have a heater at my feet
and a fine electric typer
that responds to my touch
like a lover
they are all walking by
some looking in with scorn
others with amusement

they find it humorous
thinking of the caged poet
the newest addition to the zoo
but in this case they are wrong
I was not caught or captured
I am sitting here willingly
with the rest of the world
on the other side of the glass
swimming by my fishbowl
into the darkening night

because you're fucked up and
I'm perfectly sane

I don't have to listen to you
I can cross the light
on the colour of my choice
I can wear mismatched socks
listen to Mozart one minute
and Monk the next
I can make love any time of the day or night
I can watch movies all day Wednesday
and not feel guilty
I can drink Coca-Cola at breakfast
run backwards like a dog
walk on my hands without
emptying my pockets
I can grow my moustache in three weeks
wear a ponytail to the Red Cross
I can read Proust and Popeye in the same night
I can fly when given half the chance

good morning

the house is silent
the grey cat is sleeping
and the white kitten paces the kitchen
anxious for breakfast
a mist of snow
falls outside the window

the coffee beans
have a film of oil on them
they are that fresh
as he puts them into the grinder
and the machinery turns them to dust
he puts the coffee into the percolator
with a couple slivers of cinnamon
and the percolator onto the stove
on another burner he has milk at a slow heat
while the milk and coffee warm
he halves oranges
and juices them to pulp
by the time he has poured the juice
into a small glass
the coffee is boiling
and the milk is just right
he pours the coffee into a large mug
till it is half full
then tops it with the heated milk

with both the mug and glass on a tray
he goes into the bedroom where
she has already put on red pantyhose
but is naked from the waist up
she smiles as he places the tray beside her
and the grey cat walks by their feet

10th in a series of poems from
a bookstore window

suppose you were a secret agent
or a hockey player
a cook in a Chinese restaurant
a clerk in a bank
suppose you were a stripper
or worked on the motor line at Ford
imagine you did dishes for a living
or swept the sidewalk at the Y
picture yourself pouring drinks
or making beds at a hospital
maybe you drive a truck or a bus
perhaps you wait tables at an all-night diner
imagine you were anything at all
and then picture yourself in a window
writing poems on an IBM typewriter
the poems are about any and everything
about love and losing it
about relationships and how they fail
you are not blaming anyone
but are sitting in the window
and watching the world go by
sometimes people stop and read the poems
you have taped to the window
sometimes they laugh as they walk by
you keep typing because that's what you do
you have a heater at your feet and it helps
it is not what you imagined as a child
you had dreams of being a nurse
or a fireman or a racing car driver
you envied your teachers their wisdom
and couldn't wait to grow up and be anything
other than what you are
at this exact minute

of all the poems I never planned to write

a butterfly, bright yellow
with black trim
has just spent the last ten minutes
flitting over, around and underneath
the purple and green of fragrant lilac
growing outside our kitchen window

I am reminded of poetry
I never enjoyed
delicate musings on the beauty of nature

gods of nature, forgive me
for the beauty of one butterfly
its movements pure and simple

on this morning there may be
more pressing and desperate matters
there must be

but here
for this moment at least
there is only this

Wayne Gretzky in the House
of the Sleeping Beauties

I am watching hockey on television
after all, I am a Canadian boy
but I am also reading, I am a poet too
it is a small novel by Kawabata
the story of a man who frequents a bordello of sorts
a bordello for old men only
men no longer able to have sex
they go to this house
sleep beside beautiful young women
who have been drugged and are naked
I am reading this, my eyes full of Japanese women
and lotus blossoms and then of course
that goddamned Gretzky scores, it is inevitable
he is always scoring — but I do not mind
Gretzky is an artist
I feel honoured to watch him work
I do not imagine him writing delicate Japanese prose
or taking Cecil Beaton–type photographs
like those in the book I'm holding on my lap
to use as a desk as I write this
but I am a Canadian boy and the artistry
of sticks and skates is something I understand

tonight I dream many dreams
winter and skating on a rink that never ends
in another dream I am wearing a kimono
my eyes are closed and my lips are waiting
in this dream I am thinking nipples
and the endless variety, beauty
I imagine I am with all of the girls
in Kawabata's *House of the Sleeping Beauties*
it is wonderful
and where does this all end

some incomprehensible metaphor
about hockey and Japanese women

the slash of skates into ice
like a knife into flesh
a strange version of hari-kiri

and I think no, none of these things
I watch Gretzky score another goal

in laughter and again in fear

I would smile in the direction of my uncle's demand
and in the winter we slept with our backs to the oil stove
in summer the stink of the outhouse would whisper
into the back shed where our mattress lay beneath us
I followed where he commanded
and disappeared to suit his need
on certain Sundays he would take me to the sandpit
and to prove my dedication to the others, his friends
he would force their cocks on me
I would take them and do as they asked
and when finished I would smile
hoping only for his approval and not his fist

they would laugh, slap themselves on the back
they would laugh and point
insistent in their claims that I liked it

sometimes my uncle would hang me from my ankles
over the edge of the cliff
so I could reach into the soft sand
and the holes where birds left eggs
it was all part of the game
like when he shot an acorn off my head
with a rifle
it was not by choice that I stood stone still
or lived with grandparents years beyond understanding

the nights were all the same
my uncle, big and swearing
whispering I better not ever tell
and when I cried for my parents
he would tell me to shut up
because they were never coming back

its little duck ass wobbling

you train animals for a living
there is an exhibition coming up
and someone wants a duck
wants the duck to walk up a plank
into an oven
and then lie down in a roasting pan
this is no small order
you have seven weeks
you work hard
the duck works hard
the oven is ready
you do it
you have the duck trained
it is perfect
there are three days to go
you practise
the duck comes through every time
up the plank
its little duck ass wobbling
for the reward
perfect

the night before the exhibition
the duck dies
that's the way these things work

and on the first day

you are sitting in front of the tv
eating a blt with mayo
and drinking a Coors Gold
the television is staring back at you
with gaunt faces and bloated bellies
your first reaction is anger
you had been expecting the big game
but there is a special about the millions
of starving people everywhere else in the world
you sit forward and turn the channel
only to find a program about the starved and homeless
who live only minutes from your door
you do not think about any of this
but instead try to remember the joke
your foreman told you yesterday
it had something to do with "Pakis"
and you laughed like hell
you cannot remember the joke and lean forward again
change channels hoping to catch the Lakers and Celtics
but instead the black face staring back at you
is one that has never seen a basketball
or a bacon-lettuce-tomato sandwich
it is the face of a man about your age
he holds a small bundle that looks like sticks
pieces of firewood wrapped in burlap
he is lowering the bundle into the ground
there are other bundles like it
you realize you are watching sorrow in a shallow grave
you change the channel again
but it is the same picture on every station
you take a bite of your sandwich
mayonnaise drips onto your belly
you wash the food down with beer
and wonder how the world got this way

the deer rifle

it is three in the morning and you have not slept
you are sitting in the big easy chair
facing the television you cannot hear or see
all of the lights are out so when
the big car swings into the laneway
the beams shine like a racing moon
across one wall and then another
as the caddy stops in the yard beside the willow
you know your wife is in the car and has been lying
you go to the window to see their embrace
you are not thinking about the rifle
you have in your hands
the rifle you have been cradling on your lap like a child
now you hold the rifle at your side
and then you have it levelled
it is a .303 and would blow a hole the size of an apple
through both of their skulls
there might even be a certain pride
in doing them both with one shot
you are thinking this and little else
your finger tightens on the trigger
but the traitor moon has caught the edge
of her always perfect face and it defeats you
you can no more pull the trigger
than you could jump over the damned moon
you let both the gun and your shoulders slump
step back to your chair
wait for the sound of the doors closing
first the car and then the kitchen
you hear her stumble up the stairs
you unload the rifle
leave it sitting beside the chair
you never make a sound

the painter's dream

for Daniel Sharp

a small bird flies into the studio
and cannot get its bearings to leave
it is far from home and frightened
the painter puts down his brush
and turns down the music
he is able to catch the bird
by simply distracting it for a moment

the painter carries the bird
to the table that holds his paints
and what remains of his lunch
he sets the bird down beside the sandwich
then turns, walks across the room
and opens the window wider

returning to the canvas
he occasionally glances at the bird
its blue metal body noticeably more at ease
he is not watching the bird
when it sweeps off the table
into a hard-bank right turn
then out the window

he continues to work on the canvas
occasionally looking out the window
at the ocean
calm as his heart
salt in the wind like blood
the afternoon flies by
a small joy in the larger scheme of things
one freedom leading to another

wrong number

you are in toronto to visit a friend
you are in a phone booth
and you have dialed the wrong number
an old woman's voice answers
she doesn't speak english
she says something you do not understand
and then you hear a young boy's voice
he cannot be more than ten or eleven
he speaks english well
but with an accent
he is speaking to you in one language
and to his mother in another
he politely tells you
that you have dialed the wrong number

you have no more quarters
you ask if he would do you a favour
and call your friend
you explain that you are from out of town
and that you have no more change
you give him your friend's number
and then the number of the booth
you thank him very much
and then you wait

the matador

"The sight of a man saying no with his bare hands
is one of the things that most mysteriously and
profoundly stir the hearts of men."
– andré malraux

he was sitting in the middle of the street
his pants down to his ankles
a puddle of mixed emotion at his feet
he was drunk and spinning and trying to sing
to moon the oncoming traffic

some cars honked and some flashed their lights
some of them played with him
as though he were a punch-drunk matador
eyeing up that last bull
a death grip on his sword
collapsing ass-first
onto the blacktop

later in his cell he would choke to death
two guards would come running
when the men in other cells started yelling
but the guards were not brave enough to breathe life
through the vomit that was drowning him

there would be nothing in the paper
about his death
but in the early-morning edition
under the caption "today's laugh"
a picture of him
his jacket like a cape
a sleek sports car full of life
passing by

you and your dog toto too

you are sitting on your balcony
drinking your evening beer
you see a blur pass before your eyes
a blur the exact size of a small dog
the exact size of a small dog
falling at the speed a dog would fall
thrown from an eleventh-floor window

you are unsure of what you've seen
but you have the beer and
the evening is just beginning

minutes later there is another blur
it is bigger and more vocal
you think you may even recognize
the woman who is falling
you have seen her before

what happened is:
a married couple fighting
they have a dog she likes and he doesn't
they are drinking
the dog shits on the floor
and in a drunken rage
he throws it out the window
she replies, teeth bared, red-tipped fingers slashing
so he throws her out the window too

as she falls past your balcony
you hear her screaming
and recognize her from the elevator
she is the woman who always has the dog in her arms
she always has the dog in her arms
and talks to it like a lover

the library

one son was sitting in the kitchen
the other in the living room
their mother was upstairs
we were fairly efficient
packing the boxes quickly
and with little noise
it was an amazing library
some titles in latin
others in greek
texts in spanish, french,
german and italian
he had been a renaissance man

when we started to carry
the boxes out of the house
it occurred to me
that we were carrying his history
a life devoted to literature and understanding
we had him in the boxes
as surely as if we were carrying his coffin

in the privacy of the dead man's library
we chatted about the books
the weather
about anything at all
but carrying the boxes outside
we were silent as pallbearers

loading the boxes into the truck
i felt the eyes of his family on our backs
their eyes
as we drove away

old-fashioned roller skates

it is two-thirty a.m.
you are getting a glass of water from the kitchen
or just turning off the last of the late show
you hear something outside
walk over to the window
part the curtains
and you see me
pulling a woman on old-fashioned roller skates
the ones that clamp over your shoes
their metal wheels
sound like rolling thunder on pavement
she is having a hard time keeping her balance
but being talented in matters such as this
she stays upright
as i pull her through the spotlights
of the street lamps
up and down our suburb street
then we fade into the darkness
laughing

a portrait for shaving

i remember the smell of leather and aftershave
when my father carried me on his shoulders
my hands tucked under his chin
the rough stubble of his beard amazed me
someday i would have to shave
and it made me look forward
to being just like my father

he was in the army
and had to get up very early
sometimes i'd join him
he'd put shaving cream all over my face
as if i actually had to shave
i had a plastic replica of the stanley cup
that looked like a razor
if you turned it upside down
he showed me the intricacies
of tongue in cheek to stretch the skin
how to shave under the nose

afterwards he put aftershave
on my freshly attended-to cheeks
and i watched him dress
in the meticulous razor crease
of army uniform and brass buttons

once dressed and ready to leave
he —

i remember the smell of my father's aftershave
and the way he looked standing in the mirror
but i do not remember him leaving the house
i have no memory of him coming home

fathers and sons

you are divorced
and losing your children
your wife thinks you are ill
she is taking steps
to keep you away
but today you have your son
you go to a movie
and then to mcdonald's
it is not right
she has no right
you take the boy
your son
back to your motel
tell him to watch television
while you get something out of the car
back in the room
he is lying on the bed
he suspects nothing
he is watching the roadrunner
and the coyote
the bird always wins
he is shocked when you
pour the kerosene on him
he does not understand
says nothing
the match catches
and then he is flame
you are confused
about right and wrong
you see your son on the bed
you do not hear the door
slam behind you

mrs. noah

let's say noah had a wife
a fairly understanding woman
but human, flesh and bone
noah gets the word
devotes himself to the boat
it's not like he wants to go sailing
but he's measuring cubits
drawing on the kitchen table
mumbling measurements in his sleep
their love life
dwindles to nothing
in the ensuing tedium
give or take a decade
mrs. noah takes to the grape
it starts out with thimbles
but with time and practice
she gets it down to a science

things start to go wrong
at the noah home
first it's just late dinners
but then it's no dinners at all
and then the rains
noah and his sons have been busy
but this has all been
to mrs. noah's displeasure
every day on her way to the hotel
she'd yell
"monkeys fucking in the living room
and kangaroos in the kitchen
all this shit everywhere you step
I'd rather backstroke my
way into eternity"

the big day arrives and the water is rising
noah looks around for his wife
but she is down at the local
her affair with the grape complete
noah sends his two eldest sons
to reason with their mother
and if reason fails "carry the stupid bitch home!"
the water is to their knees
as they half-drag half-carry
their screaming mother to
the boat full of beasts
and they set sail
noah and his bride
they have
lots of catching up to do

morning

someone is knocking at your door
you live in the country
and it is saturday
you do not usually
get guests at such an early hour
you do not wake up
with great speed
but once awake hear voices
and knocking
as you descend the steps
the voices outside your door get louder
they are screaming

you open the door
to two strangers
one of them a young woman
covered in blood
she is crying for help
and trying to explain
there has been an accident
the man with her is silent
he is bleeding from the top of his head

you invite them into the kitchen
and begin to tend their wounds
your husband races out to the road
to see what can be done
police and ambulance are sent for
puddles form on the kitchen floor
the sun comes up through the window

as lori-jane slept

we put her on the couch
and filled her full of drugs
then tried not to talk about it
but we were drawn to it
forced to discuss the turn in the road
and how, exactly, they cut the pole in half
we wondered how she had
walked to the farmhouse
when she had bled so badly

she told me that when she first stood up
the blood was coming so fast she couldn't see
and thought she had lost an eye
tearing off her shirt and wiping at it
until the red haze cleared

what she saw was everyone else unconscious
she dragged one guy out of the car
and he woke up
disoriented by the wheels sticking in the air
they half-carried half-dragged each other
to a stranger's door at dawn

we figured they must have been a terrible sight
semi-clad, bleeding and babbling
we watched as my sister slept
we sipped beer and watched
and it wasn't enough
we were sad for her suffering
and the suffering yet to come
the beer helping us a little
but not nearly enough
for the tears we would share when she woke
her love lying dead a hundred miles away

at the hospital

the nurse said only one of us
could go in to see her
i went first
she woke when i stood
by the side of her bed
she was covered in blood
stitches from the top of her head
to the soles of her feet
the blood a cruel mosaic
bright red
where sutured wounds still oozed
to almost black
where the blood had dried

she had no complaints
but wanted to know
about the others

there was little to tell
her boyfriend was in kingston
in intensive care
(he died the next afternoon)
her best friend was in a coma
(she died five weeks later)
the other two were released

i asked the nurse for some hot water
and a cloth
and proceeded to wash my sister
talking to her softly
with each touch of the cloth
a little more of her appeared

if not today then tomorrow

you are driving a car
and have had too much to drink
as you round a turn you realize
you are not going to make it
you feel the tires leave the pavement
as they catch on the loose sand
you hear the others
concern in their laughter
as you crank hard on the wheel
fight against gravity and other laws of nature

with some luck you get back onto the road
but going so fast you begin to fishtail
you see the road clearly
through the side window
how strange it is
to be moving this quickly, but sideways

when you leave the road for the second time
the crunch of car meeting ditch
throws you against the door
you see the telephone pole
as you race toward it
you think "isn't this strange
having the time to wish i were dreaming"
you are wishing that you are dreaming

time and your car
stop forever
the grass you have just passed over
begins to right itself
reaches up to the sun that beams down hard
and the rain it knows will fall
if not today then tomorrow

portrait

the liquor store was only three blocks from the motel
and less than a quarter of a mile
from the los angeles international airport
when the planes passed overhead walls shook
the engines screamed at full thrust
sucked the air out of the sky
but in the liquor store no one even noticed
the long grey warehouse was unpainted concrete
a no-nonsense establishment for serious drinkers
it was all on the shelves and waiting
you paid at the door
and were careful to stay away from the dog
he was tied up and waiting
for anything he could sink his teeth into
outside the heat was winning
the sidewalk was lined with lincolns and ltds
there were women in the back seats making promises
if you had the parts and the money
you'd just lean in the window and make your plans
if the price was right it was automatic
an exchange of flesh in some dark room
all conversation lost in the downpour
of the jets overhead

fade to blue

1

what i want you to see is the colour blue
a dark version
maybe like this sweater, navy
in an old-fashioned way
now forget about the fabric
you are thinking about the colour blue
and maybe a river somewhere
the river is slow-moving and dark dark blue
maybe like this sweater
the curve in the river is slow
like a dog's leg
but don't think of a dog
think of the colour blue
and the sky a lighter shade
almost another colour
you are up on a hill
and thinking that the colour blue is perfect
you are thinking it is perfect
as you lower her into the ground
you are up on a hill and thinking
that blue is the perfect colour
and between the blue sky
and the dark blue of the water
look at my sweater
this is the blue
and the light blue
almost different colour of the sky
you are thinking that between them
there are the trees
and they are fire
red orange yellow green flames
perfect to go between the blues

and you are thinking
that blue is the perfect
blue is the perfect
blue is the perfect way to describe the day
and the day is her last
as dirt is shovelled over the casket
and you walk away
into the blue horizon
fade to blue

2

if i close my eyes hard, really squint
pull my sweater over my head
it is like being under water
the fabric both rough and smooth on my nose
but i can feel that it is blue
when i close my eyes
it is like being under water
moving slowly downstream
taking off my clothes and floating
under bridges and that blue blue sky
around bends and past fields
i hear dogs barking
but my eyes are closed
i am thinking of the colour blue
shades of blue
grey blue, green blue
someone is watching me
i can feel their eyes
but i am surrounded by blue
and the blue is getting darker, darkest
where is the sky
where is the sky
i am drowning under water, blue water

am trying to pull off the sweater
i want to see the sky
i want to hear the dogs barking
i want to see the trees
on fire with colour
i can't imagine it
it is gone
only blue, dark blue
i am dead
dead
dead
and looking down on the blue water
that perfect blue
perfect in every way
this day that is my last
as the cold arms surround me
and you walk into the distance
fade to blue

summer

her room was painted white
with grey trim
there was no need for curtains
a huge tree cast green shadows
cooled the whole place down
we would lie on the bed
naked and sweating
sometimes we made love
and sometimes we didn't
it all seemed the same
the days passed without us eating
just drinking iced white wine
we were both feverish
so that when we kissed
or touched skin to skin
it was hot
and full of subtle messages
we didn't need to understand
the days passed with us together
not needing the clarification
of other people's understanding
not needing conversation
at night the street light
fought through the huge trees
and cast small leaf-sized shadows
that did not interrupt our lovemaking
the summer rambled on
and eventually fall moved in
we did not notice the passing season
but instead marvelled
at the sound of the wind
in the diminishing leaves

succubus

for terry mcevoy

you are sleeping beneath warm blankets
it is like plunging into forever
the dreams do not end and do not comfort you
you are falling into the nightmare, falling
you concentrate, it is only a dream
there is some solace in that
and you wake up shaking
happy your feet are on the ground

you are sleeping beneath warm blankets
you have played a trick on yourself and are happy
sometimes when you cannot sleep
you try to remember faces
close your eyes and draw the blankets higher
try to bring to mind the faces of women
and the warmth that you shared
you do not force anything, just let the faces come
the faces of love

you are sleeping beneath the blankets
she has you in her arms and you are frantic
this is a different type of nightmare
there is no escape, sleep provides no refuge
you do not know where   what   who you are
she has you in her arms and is pulling
pulling you deeper, into the darkness
she is perfect hell
you open your eyes to see the face of despair
and there is no one

the winnowing fan

for russell white

he was a crewcut farmer
with big arms and a sunburnt neck
he drove a 1963 fire-engine-red pontiac convertible
and he was my mother's newest flame
when winter came he was still around
but hockey didn't interest him
making it all harder to deal with

on weekends we piled into the big red car
and headed out to his family farm
i'd follow along out into the field
which was nothing like the city
there was no sense to the sun shining hot
all this long dry grass we had to throw around

when they were married
i was not allowed at the ceremony
a twelve-year-old boy
would be out of place at his mother's wedding
so i cried while the rice flew and
my mother came home
with my new father
the red convertible was gone
replaced by a grey ford that sat in the lane
beside our house and sometimes
it was a fine thing to see
when i came home from school

but with a new father
i was confused about what to do with the old one
he would show up just often enough with a small present

or a new sports car and a pretty girl on his arm
the redneck never said a word and the years passed

when mother got sick i had to go away
i was lent out to a neighbour
it was hockey season
and still he did not understand
i needed a new stick
bobby hull had just invented the curve
and every boy wanted one
when i stopped home on my way to the game
and found a new stick waiting
with just a hint of a curve
it was wrapped in white tape
and that was the first i knew
of my father

when i finally left home
knowing that i had a home to leave
made the leaving easy

now years later
i long for the hot days of summer
and an afternoon of haying
the drone of the big red tractor
and the sunburnt shoulders of the big man
throwing one bale after another
his large hands like a winnowing fan
the chafe in the whipping wind

puppies and the pissing boy

we are walking through narrow streets
looking for the statue
of the pissing boy
not nearly as amused as we were
when we found the little dogs

every few blocks
you can see a white painted stencil
of a little dog shitting
they are on the pavement
beside the sewer grates
and it is the most astonishing thing

I couldn't help but wonder
if it was one man's job alone
or if there was a crew
who roamed the late-night streets
giggling and drinking
and laying the little doggies down

we saw great paintings
and sculptures
beautiful gardens and buildings
we ate good food
and drank good wine
yet I remember the dogs
those little puppies
shitting   smiling

Brussels, Belgium

a black cat

you are in a crowded train station
where all sound is crashing down
a noisy din of language
you do not understand
being sure of nothing
you question your eyes too

you see a black cat
with one white paw
calmly whisper its way through
the maze of human limbs
as delicately with purpose
as we whisper through
the autumn leaves of our youth
pretending to be Indians, hunting
or soldiers leaving no trail

this is what you are thinking
when in the windows behind the cat
a train appears from another century
it is as black as the coal smoke will make it
and huge in the way children measure
the sound of its engine and whistle
obliterate everything in sight
obliterating even time
as you reach into your pocket
to check the ticket you cannot read
you raise your head to check on the cat
and it is gone,
memory

Pardubice, Czechoslovakia

like a painting

you are on a train
in eastern Europe
have a compartment to yourself
you are eating a sausage
with bread and mustard
you have beer you bought
at the train station
it is cold, good
every once in a while
the train passes through a village
that has lost all time
history flashes by the window
and the window becomes
an endless landscape painting
field after field after field
the land has been cleared of farmers
in a communist purge

you see an old man
walking through a field
of plowed earth
his hands behind his back
and his pace firmly set
he has a small satchel over his shoulder
and knowing he has somewhere to get to
understands that the train
is just a train
and no reason to be astonished
instead
he puts one foot in front of the other
and goes quietly
about his business

Prague, Czechoslovakia

Welsh garden

the rainbow
is azure
lilac and green
a burst of melted butter
on daffodils and dandelions
roses and tulips
fresh as painted lips
lilies bowed in prayer
radiant as innocence

at gardens end a stream
and then a forest
full of fox and ferret
owls, rats and rabbits
and then the rest of the world
everyone and everything
for as far as the mind's eye can see

St. Stephen's Green

you are sitting
in St. Stephen's Green
in the heart of Dublin
you have a good book
and the sun is shining
you can hear cars and scooters
the occasional clomp, clomp, clomp
of horses pulling carts
you are waiting for your lover
with nothing on your mind
but the grass beneath you
cool and almost damp
the sun, hot and welcome
you lie down
to be closer to the earth
closer to meaning
and discover nothing
just as you expected
a car honks
pigeons slam into the sky

Dublin, Ireland

angels in stone, angels in snow

you are hiking in South America
it has been hours since you've seen a road
or heard a voice
you are in a field
and in the middle of the field
stands a large stone
it is not any particular size or shape
but it is red, a deep red
the colour the earth would be
if enough blood were steeped into it

you walk around the stone
and are amazed to find handprints
in shades of white and grey
they look like they have been there
for all time
you place your hand on one of the prints
it is exactly the same size
as your own
the stone is warm from the sun

days, weeks, months pass
you tell no one about the hands
you are back in Canada
where snow is falling
and the late afternoon sky is dark
you are walking home
and pass through a schoolyard
beside the path you see snow angels
most are child-sized
but three are as big as you
you do not think about it
but instead flop backwards into the snow
and spread your wings

through the dark eyes of your slumber

through the dark eyes of your slumber
you hear the phone ring
and are content to let it do so
but it does not stop
minutes pass and the ringing continues
like a hammer, a bell
the gavel of the night court judge
the sound becomes clearer, crisp
ice hitting the empty glass
you feel the chill
get up to answer
and the voice at the other end
tells you your daughter's father is dead

there is silence
and then questions and details
and the electric hum
of all those miles of telephone wire
you can hear into the quiet
of all those sleeping homes
and there is no one to share this with

you find the scotch in the cupboard
and sip the prayer to another place
ask yourself over and over
"what do I tell her?"

she is sleeping
the phone did not wake her
tonight you allow her
this one final gift
a few more hours
with her father
still in her dreams

birds in the trees like madness

you are walking down a big city street
in a town that is not your own
you are beside a mental hospital
there is a park and in the park
all of the trees are bare of leaves
it is fall and almost winter
but the trees move
and you are astonished
to see they are thick with beating
the trees are alive with wings
thousands upon thousands of birds
are in the trees
and now swooping out of the sky
it is like it is raining birds
and it is only now
that you hear them
their voice one sound
loud

Gloria in excelsis deo

one of the things about my mother I really liked
was that no matter our circumstances
we never had to eat margarine
I hated margarine
and refuse to eat it to this day

my grandmother died a couple of weeks ago
she died of cancer
let me tell you what my cousin said
all six of us grandsons were pallbearers
carrying her out of the funeral home
my grandmother had never been a small woman
and my cousin and I were on the front of the box
we were the oldest
he leaned over to me as we put her in the hearse
"she sure as fuck didn't die of starvation"

when I was younger she used to give me hell
because I wouldn't eat margarine
she would demand I eat her sandwiches as prepared
bright orange greasy margarine oozing out the sides
I really don't know why I hated it so much
but I just couldn't bring myself to swallow
it didn't matter if I was turned from the table
or if she hit me or both
I just couldn't force myself to eat that shit

I remember my mother's mother having the white lard
with the blueish-purple dot for colouring
you'd bleed it into the white, white lard
the blue was dark blue, almost black
nothing like the glorious blue
of my always absent father's racing car
but blue is blue and memory holds

hunters

you are in a small plane
that whispers
just above the trees
the trees have no leaves on them
and below
you are amazed to see
dozens of hunters
in neon orange
breastplates
like confetti
in the dawn

a coral barrette from Mexico

the woman next door
lives with her seven cats
she was someone else once
with dreams
and a lover named Jerry
until an unexplained right cross
broke her nose
and her favourite vase
she'd been washing it
in the kitchen sink
when he'd approached her from behind
and drove his fist
into the back of her head
right where her coral barrette from Mexico
held her braid in place
she dropped the vase
and her nose smacked down on the faucet
she turned to see him walking away
as though he'd just kissed her cheek
as though nothing had happened

she held in her scream
and her breath
waited for him to put on his coat
and leave for work
which he did
without altering his routine
first putting on his heavy boots
and lacing them one eye short of the top
and then his scarf
always right over left, brown side up
he pulled on his leather jacket
and took his lunch
from the small table beside the door

where he knew it would be waiting
then he slipped outside
like any other day
she listened
for the sound of the car door
the engine catching, idling, then pulling away

she poured herself two fingers of scotch
drank it down
walked into the bedroom
filled her suitcase
and called a taxi
she didn't leave a note
close the door
or turn off the lights
she didn't change the answering machine
or take any books

she lives in this town now
her phone number unlisted
and she is using her mother's maiden name
you see her in the grocery store
or at the movies on a Sunday afternoon
she has short hair
seven cats
and a dog
that will tear out your heart
and leave you for dead
you can hear her calling him
every night
"come, Jerry, SIT!"

you are driving

you are somewhere between
Grand Falls and Edmundston
driving through New Brunswick
when you see a large white house
it is some distance away but straight ahead
as you near it
you gear the big truck down
instinctively turn down the radio
a voice inside, always cautious
always asking you to listen
as the air brakes hiss
as the giant clutch slows your momentum
the road has rolled down to a bridge
where the three-storey white-board house sits
on three tractor-trailer beds
dozens of men are moving hydro wires
raising them with cherry pickers and poles
after wrapping them with insulators
eventually traffic moves again
and you are back to an empty road and private world
where you sing along with Jackson Browne on the radio
a large rig blows by and you flash your high beams
when he's cleared your front end
he pulls in and flashes you a thank-you
with a double turn signal
and a blink of his back-up lights
as he pulls away

the road keeps coming at you
as you hold tight
drink Coca-Cola
chew your gum
and when you pull into Quebec
the highway opens a little

you have four lanes and no problems
it is nearing the end of the day
you've been driving since six a.m.
and you can feel the night sweep in
from the ocean like a mute tidal wave
just before all light vanishes
you see a calf on the side of the road
it is recently dead
with a huge rip through its hindquarters
you are miles past before the ghastly sleep
of the beast has fully imprinted itself
you mull over the movement of buildings
and the slaughter of cattle
the big mack groans beneath you
as you gear down for the exit
a motel and the house special
later on, you say good night
to your love on the phone
and then good night again
as you turn off the light
drink the last of your whisky
lie down to your pillow
and watch the red tip of your smoke
fade to black

hockey night in canada

for patrick hunt

early on no one scored
and it stayed like that
for the first thirty minutes
then a couple of goals snuck in
i got a beauty
there was a mad scramble
in front of the net
and it was one of those ongoing things
someone would blast it in
and the goalie would make the save
and then a defenceman
would pounce on the puck
my goal came off a rebound
i got to it first
the goalie was sprawled
and there was hardly any room
but i got it over him
and put it up on the roof
it was pretty
the game went back and forth
for some time
but as time was winding down
i got another break

i took off
and the hounds of hell could not have caught me
ed dyck flicked a soft pass
out between the two defencemen
and i was off
like i had a rocket booster in my asshole
because i was the goddamned fucking wind
i caught the puck at the red line

and the two big defenders
were right beside me
about five feet apart
but that was all
i felt a stick to each ankle
not a bad stick
or a mean stick
but a "christ, michael,
slow down!" stick
because you're going to make us look bad
it always looks bad
when the team drunk outskates someone
and i was outskating everyone
lightning wouldn't have caught me

i was skating down from centre
and in all alone
with every wish
of every boy
who ever laced a skate
i was howe and hull
béliveau and richard
paul henderson against the russians
i was bobby orr
scoring the cup winner
against the st. louis blues
george armstrong
hitting that empty net
the last time the leafs won in '67
i was gretzky and lemieux
skating down on that poor red son of a bitch
with destiny throwing me a glad hand
and a ticket to siberia
for that borscht-eating bastard

i hit the blue line
like a freight train
hitting a fruit wagon
like mario fucking andretti
hitting the gas hard
like a snake
coiled for the strike
you never see
i hit the blue line
at the speed of sound
and was gaining
on the speed of light

i heard every cheer
of every fan
from every game
from the beginning of time
and they were all on their feet
and rocking
and i may never have been good before
and i may never be good again
but i was great
flying
soaring
i was a bird
in perfect and natural grace
sweeping out and down from the heavens
whistling beethoven's fifth out of my asshole
while painting the mona lisa with my toes
i was on my back
doing what michelangelo did in the chapel
i was great caesar's ghost and then some
i was grace and beauty
and the goalie didn't have a chance

he had no more chance
than a bird in the wind
at hiroshima
no more chance
than the blonde
in the opening scene of *jaws*
just beautiful shark food
he had no more chance
than a drink
in a thirsty man's hand
i came down on him
like the charge of the light brigade
like a herd of buffalo
before the white man came
and pissed it all away
i came down on him
and made a move to my backhand
that left him and his equipment
wishing they were in another place
anywhere other than here
wishing he had someplace to hide
because this goddamned short
fucking drunk bastard
is going to kill me
he is my murderer
and my assassin
and my end and my destiny
and he is not going to leave me
anything but the memory
of the net i once protected
he is going to disgrace me
and every save i ever made
all of it wiped out
in one move
so pure and so perfect
so made for this moment

that the goalie might as well
have not been there
because this was written
before we put on our skates
before we were born
it was written
when the fish crawled out of the sea
and asked for directions

i faked to my left
to my backhand
and for all i know
the goalie is still wondering
where i went
because i went by him
like a thought
went by him
like he didn't exist
and then i put that fucker in the corner
as sweet as ali let foreman
know what destiny is all about
a little kiss to the back of the net
as sweet as dr. j
dunkin' it with his glorious, glorious beauty

i was still going fast enough
to go through the end boards
standing up
but that couldn't happen
it would all be for naught
if the ending wasn't as perfect
as the rest
i turned on a dime
as i grazed the boards
i was on rails
i was a slot car

a train
i was everything
you always dreamed i could be

in the dressing room
guys from both teams congratulated me
each sharing in what they knew
would never happen again
and each just a little pleased
to have been part of it
the goalie mentioned
that he remembered the goal
from the scramble
but not the breakaway
and i am not surprised

if i thought i was dreaming
maybe we all were
maybe it didn't happen
maybe the roar i heard
was blood pounding
in my southern comfort–cured brain
but i don't think so
i felt it
it was pure
and real
and it happened
just like i said
every word
as true as it gets

monday

another day of work
where I did what I was told

there should be some reward
for doing what you're told
most of the time I feel like anything but

today's work was more of the same
I put barcode tags on some things
and pulled them off of others

this is how my day goes
I get up in the morning and have a bath
after the bath I cover various parts of my body
with baby powder, deodorant, toothpaste, aftershave

I almost never eat breakfast
until I've been up for a couple of hours
normally a can of Coke and a joint

if there is a newspaper I read it
I usually have to use the crapper twice
once when I first get up
and once before I go out the door

on the way out I check to see
if there's any mail
always hoping for that miracle
that miracle that says
I don't have to work anymore
I don't mind work if I have to
but I'd never think of it again
if I didn't

I live downtown
so the bus is near
I take it
get off where I should
work starts
and eight or nine hours later
it ends

I get back on the bus and head downtown
at home I check the phone for messages
the fridge for a Coke
I sit at my desk and take my time
I pull out my little yellow box
take a paper from it
roll myself a treat

the smoke swirls around the room
as the day falls away
life begins
when she walks in the door

this day full of promise

let's say you're a deer
and as deer go
you're smarter than average
you're having a good year
whatever it is you like to eat
is plentiful
you've found an excellent source
of cool, clean water
your antlers are coming in
things are on target
the doe of your dreams
is doing the doe-eyed thing

it's a monday morning
although that means nothing
it is just past dawn
you don't know
that you are upwind
from the bear

this is the forest
these are the trees
the flowers are beautiful
and the air is sweet

in the city
you could be walking home
from dinner or work
you could be in your bed
under safe sheets

a man approaches
out of the darkness
neither malice nor mayhem

on his mind
he thinks no more evil
than the bear
quiet in the shadows

there is no thought
to the natural order
no safe place for the hunted

noon shines down directly
as flies skydive
the crimson puddles
the bear
having manifested its will
its reason for being
has wandered to a nearby meadow

providence has blown a beehive
from the crooked branches of an aspen
into the sweet-toothed path of the bear
there is another shaded pool
where dessert and a nap ensue
the bear dreams bear dreams
none better than reality

in the city
the closed windows of the home
you once lived in
keep in the sound of blue flies
and the answering machine's
unhappy drone

hours, days, weeks
one of them pass

you're found
by a partner, a friend
the mailman
your story is in the paper

the killer is found
or not
the sun comes up
the following day
with no regrets
and no remorse
this day
as full of promise
as every other
since the beginning of time

closer to death

I don't remember
going to bed last night
or taking off my clothes
or turning out the lights
or falling asleep
but all of them happened
and then I woke up
hungover
and closer to death
than I was
yesterday

the bar car

it was the winter of '76
the middle of the night
and the bar car was still open
we were drinking our way
across Northern Ontario
in the middle of a blizzard
I had been away
for several months

now I was headed home
without a home to head to
my drinking partner
was a little older
and a lot drunker
we'd gotten to the point
where he was slicking back his hair
by wetting his comb in his beer glass
then coiffing his locks
with a glisten of Labatt Blue

our conversation
now lost in the collective haze
of all drunken conversation

I remember only the comb
and his draining every glass in the car
before taking his leave

driving

sitting in the big truck
the engine idling
clutch on the floor
I said my driving prayer
and ground it into first
and then second
and then slowly, third
by fourth gear
the greenery started flying by
and I relaxed
found an oldies station
on the box
and pulled out a smoke

I checked my speed
ten over the limit
which was perfect
checked both mirrors
and both sides to the back
sparked my smoke
and settled in
to the black snake
laid out before me

and all those miles
yet to go

those first few weeks

I found a place
ten minutes from the factory
and spent
my first pay
at the Neighbourhood Services
buying furniture
which amazingly enough
was delivered and promptly

I remember coming home
those first few days
to strange furniture
in a new apartment
in an unfamiliar town
and just sitting on the couch
waiting to see
what would happen

no phone
and no one to phone

those first few weeks
quiet
almost lonely

where memories are made

you always thought that the worst of it
would go away
but it hasn't worked out like that
it can happen without warning
one minute you're talking with your wife or a friend
you're watching a hockey game
or a romantic comedy
where everything turns up roses
your mind is hopeful for the hero

and then you are back in time
your uncle is holding you down
ripping at your anus
with his cock

it's a white light harsh jolt
and it comes on you in an instant
like a sneeze
hangs around like a virus

you blink
hoping no one has noticed
that for a brief second
you were entirely missing
gone back in time to where
memories are made

Miles to go before I sleep

back then
when anything seemed possible
1'd think nothing
of getting into my '62 Falcon
and driving to Toronto
or Kingston
or Montreal
in the middle of the night
because there might be
a woman waiting

I liked driving at night
the window down
the shadowy night
rustling around inside the car
along with whatever music

this particular night
Miles *E.S.P.* Columbia/Legacy 65683

the days are running and then some

I've done their jobs
worked the acid bath at the car plant
with engines passing by both ears
shovelled the frozen dust of a foreman's whim
out of a northern Ontario winter
and a Falconbridge mine
drove that crazy cab full of obstinate stupidity
and the desperately sane
all night long and then some
dug that shit hole in the fly-swatting stench
of a blistering August afternoon
hammered that nail, carried that box
punched that clock

I've done all their jobs and then some
I've worked at that group home
that halfway house
I ran that hotel, drove that big truck
cut that lawn, answered that phone
typed that letter

I'm writing this now at my desk
where I'm supposed to be writing these poems
these angry, clever, minor missives
I'm sitting here all clever and stoned
it's noon on a Monday
and no job in sight

all day long

when he woke up
he remembered
she had been there

he could see her sweater
on his chair
pulled it to his face
inhaled

she was on the sweater
and it smelled good to him

he put it on
went to the kitchen
he could smell her

he went out for a walk
he could smell her

he kept the sweater on
the entire day

all day long
she came back to him

one more night

I go to her bed
knowing I want
only these moments
without past
or future

she receives me
wanting only
to change the past
reshape
her future

together
we hold hard
for the moment
imagine
we are winning

the beast
lurks
in the darkness
somewhat soothed
by our lies

in the morning
I want to leave
and she wants
me gone

sex wasn't everything to him

she asked him if sex
meant everything to him

helping her pull
her sweater over her head
he replied
that no
it wasn't

when they had changed position
for the six or seventh time
and his passion was not spent
she asked if it were
always like this
and again
he replied no

the next morning
her legs sore
her sex more so
she asked him
if this meant love
and he did not answer
but instead
stared into the ceiling
watched
as the fan turned
round and round
and round

strange fits of passion I have known

1

on the front hood of a '62 ford falcon
on a frigid suburban morning
while the sun rose over the carport

2

on a concrete beam of an incomplete bridge
while the water raced beneath us
and the mosquitoes drew blood

3

in the field beside the barn
while the bees buzzed overhead
and the long green grass tickled our thighs

the long good-morning

her hand wrapped
tightly
around his cock
is what wakes him
he didn't hear
the alarm

she is on him
working it between her lips
he thinks of the flag
and last night's dinner

she is using her tongue
he closes his eyes
and sees a painting
a large canvas
a sea of colour

she has a hand on his balls
one of her fingers
goes into his ass

he remembers a scene
from a novel
the two main characters are making it

he open his eyes
sees her head bobbing

comes

friction

he is sitting on the toilet
with his pants at his ankles
the lid on the toilet is down
she is with him
she has one hand behind his neck
and the other is cradling his balls
his cock is wet
because he's just been inside her
he slides up again
her pants are hanging from one ankle
her left shoe has knocked over a towel rack
his hands are under her ass
helping to keep the rocking steady
one of his fingers slides into her ass
it is slippery with juice from her cunt

it is four in the afternoon
and they are both working
at a small hotel
they think the place is deserted
but don't think about it much at all
both concentrating
on the inspired friction of this dancing

the poem ends when they both come

found poem

WANTED: Sexy, young female,
20–35
with full set
of upper and lower
dentures,
to help fulfill
fantasy
(nothing weird).

Generous reward
for right person.

Ottawa Citizen, May 29, 1985

the sound you hear

the sound you hear
is of a far-off train
coming slowly into town
you've heard the whistle a couple of times
you live beside the tracks
and it is early in the morning
your favourite time of the day
you are usually out of the house
before anyone is awake
you like to walk
through empty streets
see the first signs of life
a light going on in a kitchen
someone opening a door
to fetch a newspaper
how quiet everyone is
how polite
the train is edging closer
it is carrying televisions
or watermelons
or placemats
it crawls past you
and on into its train day
as the first automobiles pass by
and the street lights
go out

the dog and the idiot neighbour

standing at the kitchen window
around seven this morning
enjoying the quiet street

I see red to the southeast
and know there will be rain later

our house is quiet in the morning
a neighbour walks by with her dog

then the dog stops
and the owner with it

the owner waits patiently
while the dog lifts his hind leg

and pisses on our recycling
I figure I should say something
but am stunned silent
and immobile

the dog drops the leg
and trots off

the idiot neighbour follows
as though the animal
were the brains
of their operation

Tom

Tom was weaker than most
and when he hit it
for the last time
he didn't even see
the carpet as it raced
in fast forward
toward his already dead face

his open eyes
didn't see the television
or the dog standing over him
whining

the needle was still in his arm
when his wife found him
she turned off *Three's Company*
and put the dog
out of the room

the rest of the hour, day, week, month
evaporated
into something she would remember, later
in thirty-second clips
all prefaced with
"since Tom left"
as though he went to the corner store
for cigarettes

we brought him back across country
and buried Tom
beside an uncle he never knew

he's got all the time in the world
to get to know him now

pets

two women across the street, neighbours
almost come to blows
over the dogs of one
and the cats of the other

all human dignity surrendered
these two are reduced to threats
screaming and the scornful eyes
of every doorway within earshot

nothing is resolved
but new wounds are opened
animosities set in stone

when it is over
I slip out the side door
and into the garden
where I hunt
neighbourhood cats
with relish, gusto
and the garden hose

Friday night

you found out yesterday
that your work is ending
after eleven months
and a pretty good run

so now, mentally
you're gearing up again
all those phone calls
to make
all that waiting

you're getting too old
for manual labour
you can do the work
but pay for it every night
with aching ankles
sore back

you're no longer the young optimist
one job promises to be much like the next
your time for their money

and that is how it goes
your present job ends
a week from Friday
you're already thinking ahead
to the first Friday of freedom
from the job you've yet to find

the future waltzes in
like it knows your name
settles into the corner
a quiet spider

saying goodbye to Pardubice

my nose was broken, I was sure of that
I'd broken it a few times before and remembered
how tight my face felt, like a balloon

one or two ribs were busted as well
it was hard to tell with the adrenaline pumping
fear and anger jacking up the levels

fear conquers reason and sometimes
it is the other way around
either way I had to leave town
and quickly

the coward in me packed a shoulder bag
with ice-cold beer and took a cab
to the station

the three young soldiers in my compartment
didn't say a word about my blackened eyes
and distended face
but politely thanked me
as we bargained down the beer

I hated leaving and I hated being a coward
but all these years later
I'm happy to be alive

2 Charles Dickens, 1 Brautigan

the river is black
where it is not covered with snow
a set of tracks
lead to open water
head only
in one direction

on the shore
is a small suitcase
with an envelope inside
there are three books
and a photo album

the photo album
has infant photos
grade school
and some high school shots
from then on
sporadic snaps
of family gatherings
and little else

missing are friends
a lover
a club

his phone book
is mostly blank
his apartment
mostly empty

there is so little
to this old story
called lonely

the front porch

she sits on the small front porch
reading one of those softcover summer novels
I'm just inside, at the table, reading as well
and now doing some writing

we are in a small village, Magpie
on the north shore of the Gulf of St. Lawrence
about fifteen or twenty
small homes dot the rocky shore
this house is owned by a friend

the fog is rolling in or out
every time I turn my head
one minute the large rocks
two hundred yards from shore
are clear and imposing
seconds later, the rocks and all else
vanish into the milky grey haze

without her, the one on the porch
the same thing happens to me
my clarity and certainty vanish
I lose dimension, shape, substance
you can see right through me

my lucky life

woke up early this morning
and came downstairs
to a blazing sun
and a horizon of blue on blue
at about six-fifteen
I saw a whale

I've seen them before
but never from the kitchen window
while sitting in a chair
at the table

for most of my life
I have only had a
minor connection with nature
I live in a big city
and do big-city things
but here on the edge of the ocean
I get to share a bit
of that other real world
and am reminded once again
how small I am

all the beauty
in my lucky life

goodbye

it was a warm night
and when I pulled into the laneway
I could see her in the window
and then at the door

she came out of the house
without slippers or shoes
I noticed how tiny her feet were
how wide awake her smile

it was the middle of the night
I'd already driven a couple hundred miles
and had a few hours more to go
this was strictly a pit stop

she invited me into her parents' home
where I met them
after disturbing their sleep
they returned to bed
while she and I talked on the couch
our conversation took us back
to our first and only
other meeting
all heat and summery passion

we held hands then kissed
I had to be in another town by morning
and morning was getting closer
we said goodbye in the living room
my hands working their way under her gown
we said goodbye again in the kitchen
as she put her hands into my pants

once outside we said goodbye
for the last time
her perched on the hood
of my 1963 metal-flake-blue Ford Falcon
and me between her legs
the two of us gasping
goodbye, goodbye, goodbye

somewhere further up her street
a man rolled over in his sleep
put his arm on his wife's shoulder
and she inched away

in another home
the family dog ate out of the cat's dish
a goldfish swam silent circles
through a steady hum of bubbles

fours hours to the east
the sun was coming up
over other laneways, other parked cars
over the Atlantic ocean
over boats
and seagulls
and the horizon
that stretches
all the way to the future

out of sight

the silly thing about pens
is the way they write
affects what you write
people might not want to believe such things
but it is true

Shelley's poems
sound like they were written
with a quilled nib

Brautigan's with a pen
that used only the ink
from an albino octopus

Sexton clearly wrote in elegant lipstick
and Bukowski
in beer and blood

with my poems
it doesn't matter as much

pencil, pen, typewriter
it's all the same
this far under water
this far out of sight

my mother made me

my mother made me
because she was fifteen
and alone in the back seat
with a young man
in a starched uniform
she had a teenage heart
and a grown woman's desire
she wasn't thinking about me
when she made me
she was thinking
that this is the future
that this man
will make it so
when my mother made me
she was thinking of leaving home
of plumbing
and matching kitchen chairs
she was thinking of that altar
that uniform
that honeymoon

filing cabinet

called one bank to complain
about their late-night phone calls
and a $20 service charge
called another to increase
our line of credit

boiled four eggs
peeled them
and set them beside
one dill pickle
and a slice of buttered
whole wheat bread

two phone calls this afternoon
and both were wrong numbers
received an email
asking me to do a reading
and they promised money

of course I'm out of town
the night of the reading
out of the country as well

watched a movie about family
thought about my own

found some ants beneath the kitchen window
put down some goo
it kills them, their friends
their friends' families
I am the Keyser Söze
of ants in the kitchen

put away papers
from one file to another
then into my filing cabinet
where no one goes but me

no secrets, but the details
of my tired little life
in that box, this poem

another history lesson

now I'm at another museum
and yesterday I packed up a dress
that had belonged to a French woman
during the Second World War
it was from a German prison camp

I lined it with acid-free tissue paper
and made careful rolls for the sleeves
I gave it as much reverence as I could muster
as I lay it into a box
copied the documentation three times

one for inside the box
one for outside the box
and the third for our files

I put the box in the appropriate pile
and moved on
to another
piece of history

career choice

there are monuments to poets everywhere
Mayakovsky has streets named after him
Pushkin is a patron saint

the statues of poets
are as big as those of Lenin
or any of the generals

what a strange world
that they love what I love
while in my part of the world
what I love is invisible

poets less popular
than the garbage man
who admittedly
provides a more obvious
and perhaps more necessary
service

the next time
someone important dies
and needs to be commemorated
maybe you should call
the garbage man

after all
eventually
he will take it all
away

Moscow, Russia

writing

I want to dig right into the page
with my pen
and come out with
what's underneath

when watching a movie
you always know
the fate of the hero
but I want the details
on the guy who opened the door
or served the dinner
or parked the car

I wonder how his life turned out

the finishing work
and the bus ride home
a beer and a shower
maybe something classical
on the stereo
while he goes to the fridge
finds a cucumber
the thawed steak
he removed from the freezer that morning
he chops an onion and sips his beer
the music hits a crescendo

he opens a cheap red with dinner
eats in front of the television
likes sports, watches the news
but tonight it's a game show
"what is the Bermuda Triangle, Alex?"

I pull back from the page
I've discovered nothing of importance
about the man or myself
and am reminded
of what George Armstrong
once told me
not the George Armstrong
who scored into an empty net
the last time the Leafs won the Cup in '67
but the George Armstrong I knew
the one who'd served twenty-five years
for shooting his bank manager

I asked him about those twenty-five years
he spent behind bars
and he replied:
"no astonishing remarks"

and so I wondered how many of us
live lives of no importance
our coming and going
no more significant
than an ant crawling up a sunflower
and back down again
and with that
the poem is over

until I thought
it might not have been important to George
but I'm pretty sure
the bank manager's family
thought it was important
astonishing even

it wasn't my first reading

it wasn't my first reading
but my first in a while
and certainly my first in a sex shop

it was in a building
that used to be a laundromat
run by a veteran of the Vietnam war
he was a deeply disturbed
and angry man
the laundromat was always in disarray
but we did our cleaning there
from time to time

I'd fill my pockets with quarters
then fill the machines
whites in one washer
colours in another
I'd take a book to read
each load good for a chapter
but in all those warm hours
it never occurred to me
the space would become
a designer-dreamed woman-friendly porn palace
or that I would launch a book in it

it required me writing a book of erotic poems
which I did

recently, at a party
a woman who'd read my book
took exception to one of the poems
and grilled me about it
she didn't object to the cock/cunt stuff
or tongues in asses

no, her distress
was over a French Eskimo kiss
which only goes to show
she needed to travel more

the launch itself was a blur
every time I looked up from the page
the smiling faces of the crowd
were framed by a wall of enormous dildos
dildos of every length, thickness and colour
all of them reminding me of my shortcomings
I'd look up and see the audience
watching me
the harnesses and belts and sex swings
lined up behind them like piñatas
waiting for the party to start

Boxing Day

Boxing Day required a short excursion
to the local variety store
about four blocks from our door

in those four blocks
I saw three girls
it seemed
they were working

our short street is an oasis
in our part of town
a nice house
a nice garden
and we are the lucky ones

at the corner store, Mikey's
one of the girls
is struggling through her purchase
buying penny candy
although nothing costs a penny anymore

the Iranian clerk, Shardad
has asked her to put a plastic bag
over her hand
as she reaches into the bins
and she does so
knowing the obvious
but unstated truths
it is a difficult transaction to witness
a sad opera
she is stoned to distraction
almost putrid with perfume
and the dull stale stink of crack

and when she is finished and gone
Shardad apologizes to me

I tell him
there is no reason
and I pay for my loaf of bread

out on the street
I see the candy girl
saunter to her station
on the corner

she looks me up and down
as she pops
a jawbreaker
eyes me the invite

I smile politely
and continue
on my Boxing Day way
back to our quiet enclave
Nat King Cole on the box
lights twinkling
on the tree

the pest

we were spending the month of August
in Italy
most of it with family
a mistake
I won't make again

on this particular day
my wife and I
found ourselves
getting off a train
six hours early
and in a town
that had closed its doors

we dragged our luggage
up one side
of an abandoned street
and down the other

it was over 40 celsius
and I could feel
pieces of me
falling off in the heat

I had wanted a ride to our destination
some miles yet to go
but for reasons of convenience
and a bit of family bile
we were taken to a station
miles from our destination
and left to survive the heat
in the blast furnace of the day

the skin on my feet
peeled off in protest
as I dragged our Air Canada bags
along the melting promenade

eventually we found a café
with cheap wine and cold water

I knew, somewhere down the line
I'd appreciate family once again
and hopefully they'd feel the same about me
but I knew it wouldn't be this summer
I knew it wouldn't be soon

the wine and water helped
but not enough

my wife saw it another way
and she was angry with me
so she buried her face in a book
and tolerated me
like a mosquito
she wasn't quite mad enough
to swat

pork pie hat in a minor chord

ever since I saw a photo
of Lester Young in a pork pie hat
I've wanted one of my own

Charles Mingus wrote
"Goodbye Pork Pie Hat"
with Joni Mitchell

Porky Pig wore a pork pie hat
and the irony of that
cracks me up

Dexter Gordon
Charlie Parker
all those cats
they wore them

now
I've got one
still no connection
between me
and the greats

but
hell if I don't like
tipping my hat

stars on the ceiling

I can hear them
my poems
working away
in the back
of my skull
like sirens
and that
is what night
has become

sirens
coming and going
in the distance
but none
coming close enough
to see

two cats
meet in a yard
nearby

a dog smells them
through a screen door
his bark
echoes
down the street
as imagined stars
arc slowly
over the skyscape
of my ceiling

on being a dodo

another way to think
about the end of the world
is to not think about it at all
forget I mentioned it
or that it is even possible

remember the Academy Awards
and the winner of the Kentucky Derby
listen to John Tesh sing duets with Céline Dion
watch gladiators fight on television
have a pizza delivered
plan a Mexican holiday

you are not alone
our demise is no careful plan
but rather
the final proof
that Darwin was right
that dodo
really didn't know
his time was up
he died without worrying
that he was the last of his kind
most of us
we won't be
so lucky

he was just dead

when my father died
I was expecting
some sort of revelation
a deeper understanding
of something, anything
some sort of Dead Father Bonus
but instead
he was just dead

we hadn't talked
there had been nothing to settle
to him I'd lost my mind
in unjustifiable anger

I'd quit trying
when I finally realized
he wasn't listening to me

and it was never
about a particular conversation
but rather
that he couldn't hear
my music

when I realized
I was only talking to myself
when he was in the room
I left

it was seven years later
that he passed away
in a distant hospital room

I hadn't said a word

your child

what if someone stole your child
it doesn't matter how it happens
it could be at a supermarket
when you've turned your head
or at school during recess
the details don't matter
only that your child is missing

the police have been down this road
and suspect everyone including you
having nothing to hide
you speak to the press
and with your innocent tongue
say whatever comes into your mind
why wouldn't you?

while somewhere else
in the same town
a man and woman
sit down to supper
they eat
while watching a game show
on television
they are concentrating
on the television

they know what has happened
in a way no one else does
during a commercial
she goes to the fridge
brings them another beer
when a news update
appears on screen
they change the channel

you are at your home
insane with grief
incapable of anything
you demand the impossible
of yourself
you manage stoic in public
you do it for your child
the way you carry yourself
becomes the news

your child is still missing
the day-long hours
the century-long days
drag you unceremoniously
to the darkest place on the planet

the death of your child

all public doubt
removed from your shoulders
no respite at all
as her death
rains down around you
and it pours
and pours
and pours
all the sad future
without her

hangover

earlier this morning
two crows were
holding court on our street
what they were arguing about
will have to remain a mystery
because you know crows
they'll never stop talking
but they'll never tell

the crack-the-silence caw
of their black bleating
nearly blinds a hungover man
and they'd found one

last night I followed
Portuguese red table wine
with a few Czech friends
and what was an interesting conversation last night
is more than a language problem this morning

only mother nature
could be this cruel
kindly giving us
the grape and hops
and the visions of excess to go with them

then the hard cold call
of the cawing crow
like harsh sunlight
right in the eyes
all that clarity
so temporary
as the white light
begins to flash

small miracle

A harbour filled with ships and no one sailing
anywhere. There had been a flash freeze sometime
the previous night. Now the harbour was black glass,
smooth as the surface of a mirror.

Those who were awake were abnormally quiet: no
sound of water lapping, waves waving or anyone
waxing eloquent. Instead the whisper of voices
soft-breathed over glass.

You knew it couldn't last but nonetheless it was
spectacular. Like the earth had gone to sleep for a
moment and left us all in silence.

Mothers stirred in their beds but did not rise.
Children awoke but did not cry out. Most peculiar, in
a harbour, was the silence of birds. Not a sound.

The wind blew clouds of powdery snow like cotton-
candy sentinels against the wooden sides of the
sibilantly silent ships.

And then, from the east, the sun crested the hills
that hid the harbour, and something no one had
ever seen before: a horse, unexplainably loose
and walking slow-footed over the harbour, toward
the sea.

the best second ever

Jan Garbarek screaming through his sax
for some sort of Urdu logic

I'm listening to this
as waves crash against Côte-Nord
a beautiful symmetry
Qawwali music and the constant slap
of the ocean hitting the shore

and as Jan approaches a vocal ecstasy
his saxophone takes wings
somewhere over the St. Lawrence
and Nusrat Fateh Ali Khan
slingshots him out of the sky
with a vocal response
that is colour reimagined

they cartwheel each other
toward an emotional nirvana
neither expected
nor fully comprehended

but it is there
like every flower
from every bloom
in all the world
bursting into the flame
of full splendour
in one moment

Allah, God, Vishnu
man woman
all the rest
be praised

the little woman

I weigh almost 220 most days and am a short man
I flatter myself when I describe my build as fire hydrant
I'm really more like Winnie the Pooh

in a week or so I'll be 54 and over the years
I've broken bones, had operations
been exposed to pain of all sorts
physical, emotional and the other kinds

but nothing is quite like the blackfly bite
my calf has been throbbing for three full days
and I have hot rocks under my skin

my wife isn't laughing, at least not to my face
she has a couple of bites as well
but they seem to have no more effect on her
than a bad commercial on TV
my wife, she is not a complainer
I remember a trip when she broke one of her toes
but we were in Paris so she walked on it anyway
her sock bloody at the end of the day
she didn't even say boo

me, belittled by the smallest black bug
my reasonable wife swatting them away with
nary a care in the world

the world equally in love
with us and the blackflies
and the brown stone
and the white sand
and the red ants
who build giant cities
under the ground

ACKNOWLEDGEMENTS

The "Selected" poems previously appeared, in earlier versions, in these books and chapbooks:

quarter on it's edge: curved light; funeral for a fly; sparrow, again; april 29 1979; tournesol

sometimes passion, sometimes pain: i share an apartment with two artists; why i don't like fellini; in the glass

no saviour, no special grace: breakfast in bed; no saviour and no special grace; where the water tastes like wine

how to keep a poet out of jail – or ship of fools, car of idiots: dinner; the first night; Nancy's perfect little gun

poems for Jessica-flynn: fishbowl; because you're fucked up and I'm perfectly sane; good morning; 10th in a series of poems from a bookstore window

wayne gretzky in the house of the sleeping beauties: of all the poems I never planned to write; Wayne Gretzky in the House of the Sleeping Beauties; in laughter and again in fear; its little duck ass wobbling; and on the first day; the deer rifle; the painter's dream

Fade to Blue: wrong number; the matador; you and your dog toto too; the library; old-fashioned rollers kates; a portrait for shaving; fathers and sons; mrs. noah; morning; as lori-jane slept; at the hospital; if not today then tomorrow; portrait; fade to blue; summer; succubus; the winnowing fan *what we remember and what we forget:* puppies and the pissing boy; a black cat; like a painting; Welsh garden; St. Stephen's Green

missing the kisses of eloquence: angels in stone, angels in snow; through the dark eyes of your slumber; birds in the trees like madness; Gloria in excelsis deo; hunters; a coral barrette from Mexico; you are driving

no gravy, no garland, no bright lights: hockey night in canada; monday; this day full of promise

All Those Miles Yet to Go: closer to death; the bar car; driving; those first few weeks; where memories are made; Miles to go before I sleep; the days are running and then some

Arrows of Desire: all day long; one more night; sex wasn't everything to him; strange fits of passion I have known; the long good-morning; friction; found poem

Coming Ashore on Fire: the sound you hear; the dog and the idiot neighbour; Tom; pets; Friday night; saying goodbye to Pardubice; 2 Charles Dickens, 1 Brautigan; the front porch; my lucky life; goodbye; out of sight; my mother made me; filing cabinet; another history lesson; career choice; writing; it wasn't my first reading; Boxing Day; the pest; pork pie hat in a minor chord

Watching the Late Night Russian News in the Nude: stars on the ceiling *on being a dodo:* on being a dodo; he was just dead; your child; hangover

how are you she innocently asked: small miracle

The Uncertainty of Everything: the best second ever; the little woman

THE AUTHOR THANKS:

Without Stuart Ross this book wouldn't have happened, and I am forever in his debt. Bruce McEwen's support and encouragement has been a generous gift. Christian McPherson has been a bigger help than he knows. I would like to thank Brian Kaufman and the Anvil team for everything. And K, who I can never thank enough.

THE EDITOR THANKS:

Bruce McEwen, who somehow conjured up electronic copies of most of these poems, at no small effort. Sarah Moses, who offered valuable feedback on the introduction. Michael Dennis, whose decades of friendship and poetry talk and collaboration have made my life better.

Born in London, Ontario, in 1956, **Michael Dennis** published his first poems in the early '70s. His working life has included everything from stints in car plants and copper mines to installing artworks in galleries and doing time as a short-order cook and a dishwasher in a strip club; he ran a small boutique hotel in the '80s, was Santa at the Kmart in Charlottetown one year, and opened a non-profit ESL school in Jablonec nad Nisou, Czechoslovakia, immediately following the Velvet Revolution. Michael has driven a taxi and a truck and had a brief stint as a private chauffeur. Now semi-retired, he lives in Ottawa, where he writes the popular blog *Today's book of poetry*.

Stuart Ross is the author of nearly twenty books of poetry, fiction and essays. He has edited hundreds of books, including *Why Are You So Sad? Selected Poems of David W. McFadden* (Insomniac Press, 2007), *Book of Short Sentences*, by Alice Burdick (Mansfield Press, 2016), and *Certain Details: The Poetry of Nelson Ball* (WLU Press, 2017). For a decade, Stuart had his own imprint, a stuart ross book, at Mansfield Press. In fall 2017, he launches A Feed Dog Book, at Anvil Press. Stuart lives in Cobourg, Ontario.